Hairy, Scary, Ordinary

What Is an Adjective?

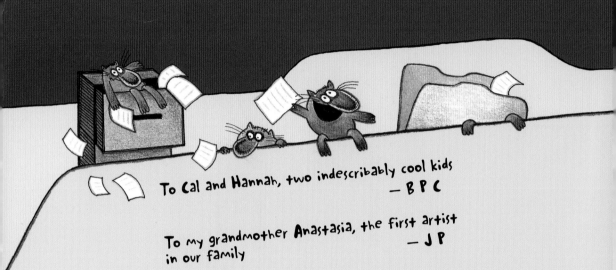

To Cal and Hannah, two indescribably cool kids
— B P C

To my grandmother Anastasia, the first artist
in our family
— J P

adjective: A word that describes a thing, idea or living being.

Hairy, Scary, Ordinary

What Is an Adjective?

by Brian P Cleary

illustrated by Jenya Prosmitsky

LERNER BOOKS · LONDON · NEW YORK · MINNEAPOLIS

Adjectives are words like hairy,

Scary, cool and ordinary.

They describe,
like tan
and tall,

Funny, frisky,

smooth and small.

5

They tell us
things
are

orange
or
green,

Hot or cold
or in-between,

Leaky,

Squeaky,

ancient,

new,

Easy,

breezy,

broken blue.

7

Adjectives help tell us more,

Like narrow street or favourite toy store,

KOOL KITTY TOYS

EXIT

8

Hilly, chilly, fast and fun, undercooked and overdone.

9

They tell us of an old black boot,

A rainy day, a Wrinkled suit,

A silly teacher, giant hair,

A large cow at the local fair —

Footballs that are red and rubber,

Spot's clean fur each time you scrub her,

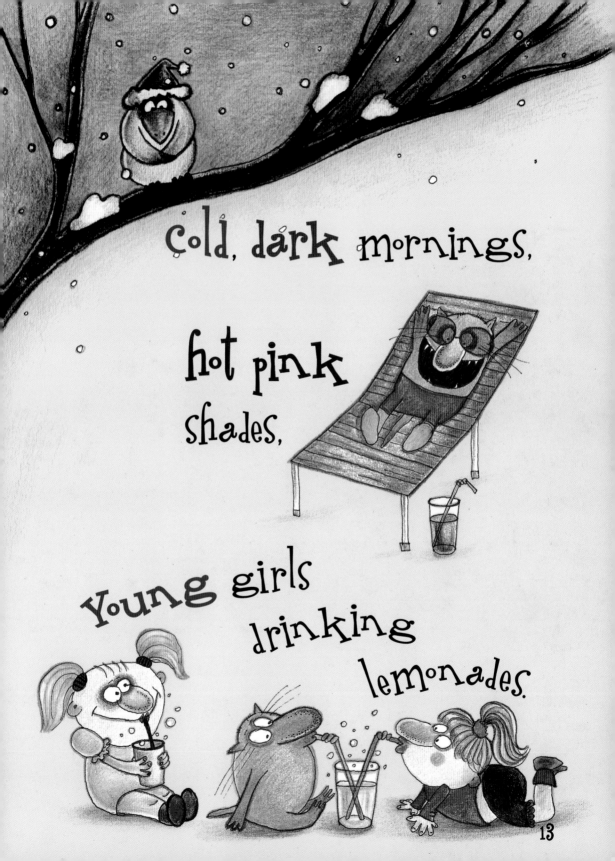

cold, dark mornings,

hot pink shades,

Young girls drinking lemonades.

13

They tell if your drink is *flat* or **fizzy**,

And if your street is **quiet** or **busy**,

That treats
are yummy,

shakes are
thick,

And if your
tummy's calm
or sick.

They're colourful, like **mauve** and puce,

They help explain, like lean and loose,

99% FAT FREE

Baggy, saggy,

stretchy, strong,

Much
too short

or way too long.

Adjectives are words like flashy,

Vibrant, bright and somewhat trashy,

Frilly,
silly,

polka-dotted,

single-looped

or

double-knotted.

19

Words like
Spunky,

rather clunky,

Priceless, nice

or downright funky,

Speedy, Spoiled,

Spiffing, Spare,

Thrifty, nifty,

bronze and bare.

THE FOOT MICHELANGEL-TOE

They **modify** nouns
in ways that help tell us

If
someone's
Sincere,

delighted or **jealous,**

If jackets are herringbone, pinstriped or checked,

If babies are crabby, excited or perfect.

They tell us that TV is stupid or funny,

of books that are stuffy, amazing or punny,

Of looks that are **frightening**,

dogs that are **stray**,

Of coffee that's **black**

in a cup

that is **grey**.

Adjectives help us describe when we're **tired,**

Or say when we're **grumpy,**

or when we are **wired.**

Without 'em we couldn't tell Mum how we feel,

Like hungry, or hurting or ready to squeal.

27

Lopsided, one-sided ball games that bore us,

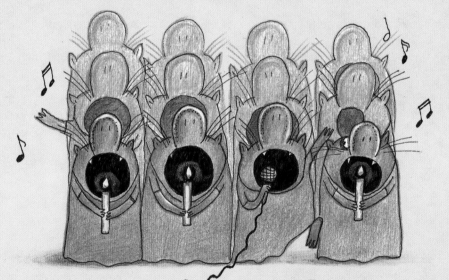

The sweet, gentle sounds that descend from the chorus,

Mighty blue oceans and tiny red rings.

Adjectives tell us of all of these things.

29

So, what is an adjective?

Do you know?

ABOUT THE AUTHOR & ILLUSTRATOR

BRIAN P CLEARY is the author of the best-selling Words Are CATegorical™ series and the Math is CATegorical™ series as well as Peanut Butter and Jellyfishes: A Very Silly Alphabet Book, Rainbow Soup: Adventures in Poetry and Rhyme and PUNishment: Adventures in Wordplay. Mr. Cleary lives in Cleveland, Ohio, USA.

JENYA PROSMITSKY grew up and studied art in Chisinau, Moldova. Her two cats, Henry and Freddy, were vital to her illustrations for this book.

First published in the United State of America in 2000

First published in the United Kingdom in 2009 by
Lerner Books,
Dalton House,
60 Windsor Avenue,
London SW19 2RR

Website address: www.lernerbooks.co.uk

This edition was updated and edited for UK publication by Discovery Books Ltd., Unit 3, 37 Watling Street, Leintwardine, Shropshire, SY7 0LW

British Library Cataloguing in Publication Data

Cleary, Brian P., 1959-
Hairy, scary, ordinary : what is an adjective?. - 2nd ed. -
(Words are categorical)
1. English language - Adjective - Juvenile poetry
I. Title
425.5

ISBN-13: 978 0 7613 4271 7

Printed in China